Got Game

FOOTBALL SUPERSTARS

Nicki Clausen Grace
and Jeff Grace

WORLD BOOK

This World Book edition of *Football Superstars*
is published by agreement between
Black Rabbit Books and World Book, Inc.
© 2018 Black Rabbit Books,
2140 Howard Dr. West,
North Mankato, MN 56003 U.S.A.
World Book, Inc.,
180 North LaSalle St., Suite 900,
Chicago, IL 60601 U.S.A.

Jennifer Besel, editor; Michael Sellner, designer;
Omay Ayres, photo researcher

Library of Congress Control Number: 2016049953

ISBN: 978-0-7166-9318-5

Printed in the United States at CG Book Printers,
North Mankato, Minnesota, 56003. 3/17

BOLT

Image Credits

Alamy: Jason O.Watson, 20
(players); ZUMA Press, 17 (bottom);
AP Images: Aaron M. Sprecher, 1, 16,
Back Cover; Darron Cummings, 25; Mark
Zaleski, 24 (Step 1 and 2); Matt Patterson, 14, 26
(punter); SCOTT AUDETTE, 13; Newscom: Anthony
Nesmith, 18 (Brady); Jim Dedmon, 18 (Kuechly);
Shutterstock: Alesandro14, 10–11 (field); Dimec, 10–11
(players); EsraKeskinSenay, 3, 10–11 (lights), 18–19
(lights), 24–25 (lights); Svyatoslav Aleksandrov, 31;
VitaminCo, 7, 20 (football), 26 (football), 28 (football),
32; USA Today Sports: Brad Penner, 19 (Revis); Geoff
Burke, Cover, 9; Jim O'Connor, 18 (Beckham); Kelvin
Kuo, 28–29; Kirby Lee, 19 (Vinatieri); Kyle Terada, 6;
Mark J. Rebilas, 4–5, 17 (top); Michael Hickey, 23;
Troy Taormina, 19 (Watt)
Every effort has been made to contact copyright
holders for material reproduced in this
book. Any omissions will be rectified
in subsequent printings if notice is
given to the publisher.

Contents

CHAPTER 1

Working

for the Win

It was the 2015 Super Bowl. The Patriots were down by 10 points. Tom Brady didn't give up. He threw powerful passes. His team won.

In 2017, another Super Bowl win seemed impossible. The Patriots were down by 25 points. But Brady did it again. He launched passes. And the Patriots came back for the win.

Football superstars have skills and **confidence**. They do what it takes to win.

CHAPTER 2

Offensive Players

Offensive players move the ball down the field. They battle other teams' **defenses**. And they make touchdowns.

Tom Brady is a quarterback for the New England Patriots. He has led his team to five Super Bowl wins. He also led his team in the NFL's longest winning streak.

Brady has thrown more than 400 passing touchdowns.

Odell Beckham Jr.

Odell Beckham Jr. seems to catch impossible throws. He is a wide receiver for the New York Giants. In his first two seasons, he had 2,755 **receiving yards**. No other player has had that many in their first two seasons.

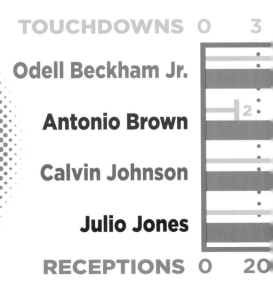

Comparing Wide Receivers' First Two Seasons

TOUCHDOWNS 0   3

Odell Beckham Jr.

Antonio Brown

Calvin Johnson

Julio Jones

RECEPTIONS 0   20

6   9   12   15   18   21   24   27   30

25

87

85

16

126

18

133

40   60   80   100   120   140   160   180   200

Offense

offensive line ·····

wide receiver

quarterback

running backs

wide receiver   tight end

Defense

defensive line

linebackers

defensive backs

defensive back

Todd Gurley

Todd Gurley made a splash his **rookie** year. He ran for 1,106 yards in just 13 games. He is a 227-pound (103-kilogram) running back. He is known for his speed and power.

Gurley was the 2015 Offensive Rookie of the Year. He also went to the Pro Bowl his first year. Fans can't wait to see what he does next.

Gurley had a knee injury during the 2015 draft. The Los Angeles Rams still picked him in the first round.

CHAPTER 3

Defensive
Players

The defense blocks the other team from scoring. Defensive players tackle and try to steal the ball.

J. J. Watt is a defensive end for the Houston Texans. He has made more than 75 **sacks**. He's known for his leaps.

Luke Kuechly

Players have to be quick to spot Luke Kuechly. He moves all over the field. Kuechly is a linebacker for the Carolina Panthers. He played in four Pro Bowls.

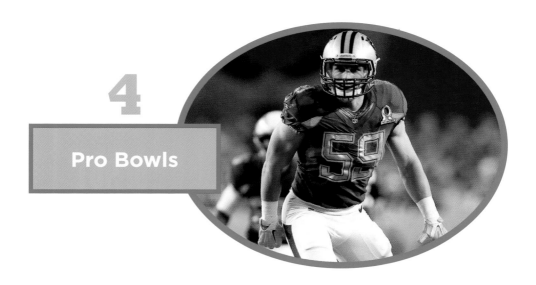

4

Pro Bowls

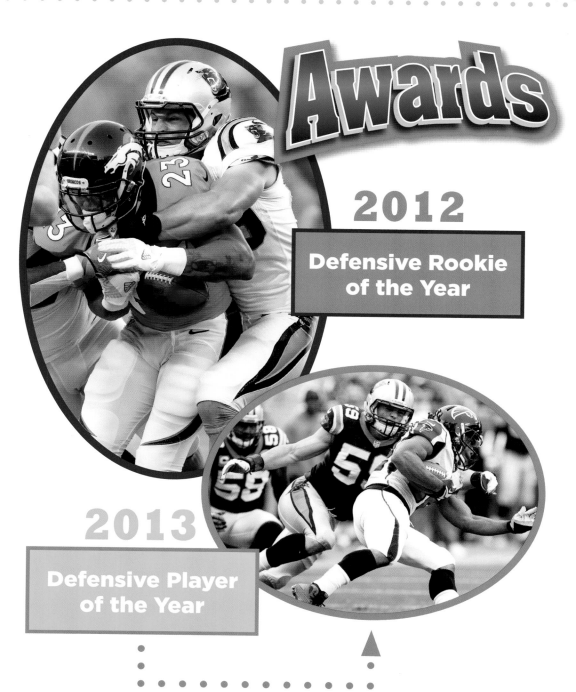

Awards

2012
Defensive Rookie of the Year

2013
Defensive Player of the Year

17

SIZE THEM UP

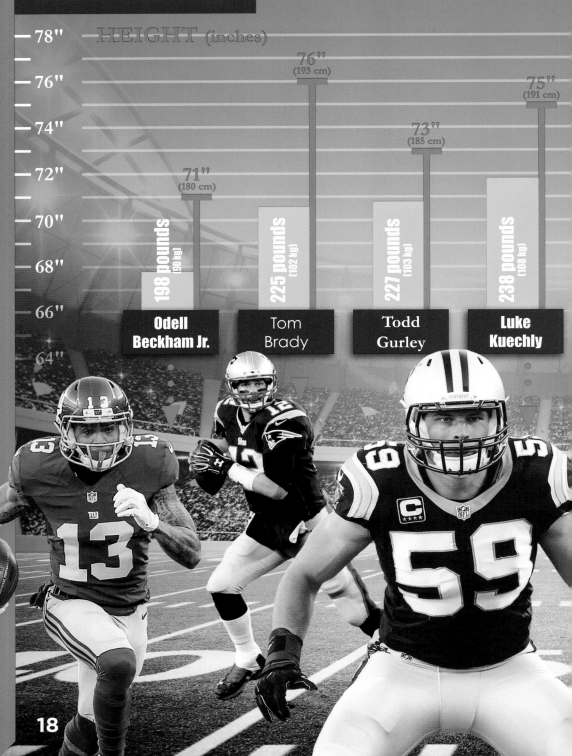

HEIGHT (inches)

78"
76"
74"
72"
70"
68"
66"
64"

71"
(180 cm)

76"
(193 cm)

73"
(185 cm)

75"
(191 cm)

198 pounds
(90 kg)

225 pounds
(102 kg)

227 pounds
(103 kg)

238 pounds
(108 kg)

Odell Beckham Jr.

Tom Brady

Todd Gurley

Luke Kuechly

WEIGHT
(pounds)

300
290
280
270
260
250
240
230
220
210
200
190
180
170
160

74"
(188 cm)

71"
(180 cm)

72"
(183 cm)

77"
(196 cm)

230 pounds
(104 kg)

198 pounds
(90 kg)

206 pounds
(93 kg)

295 pounds
(134 kg)

Shane
Lechler

Darrelle
Revis

Adam
Vinatieri

J. J.
Watt

Revis'
Career
Interceptions

2007	2008	2009
3	**5**	**6**

Darrelle Revis

Darrelle Revis is known for stopping plays. He is a cornerback for the New York Jets. Revis is a seven-time Pro Bowler. He has made more than 25 **interceptions** in his career.

2010	2011	2012	2013	2014	2015	2016
0	4	1	2	2	5	1

CHAPTER 4

Special Teams

Special teams players can be game changers. Punters and kickers only play when the ball should be kicked. The pressure is on when they take the field.

Adam Vinatieri is the oldest player in the NFL. He's a kicker for the Indianapolis Colts. He is the only player to score more than 1,000 points for two different teams.

Vinatieri has made two different game-winning Super Bowl kicks.

KICKING THE BALL

Center snaps the ball to the holder.

Holder places ball on the ground and holds with one finger.

Step 1

Step 2

Kicker takes······
steps toward
the ball and
kicks.

Field Goal!

Lechler's Yards Per Punt Averages
2010-2015

2010
47.0

2011
50.8

2012
47.2

2013
47.6

2014
46.3

2015
47.3

Shane Lechler

Shane Lechler is a punter for the Houston Texans. He has played in seven Pro Bowls. He's played more games in a row than any other active NFL player.

Pro Players

Football superstars amaze fans with their moves. They make people stand up and cheer. Without great players, football wouldn't be the same.

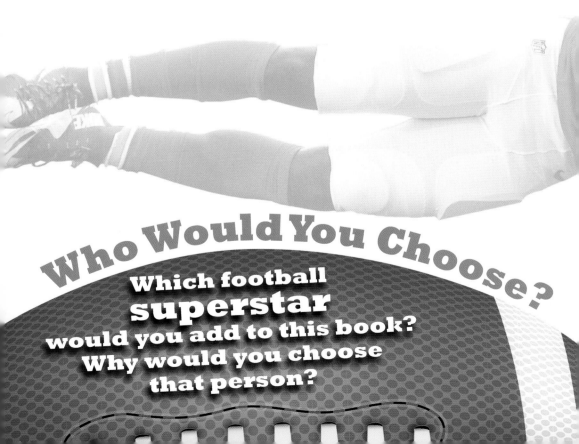

Who Would You Choose?

Which football **superstar** would you add to this book? Why would you choose that person?

GLOSSARY

center (SEN-tuhr)—a football player in the middle of the offensive line who passes the ball behind him to start the play

confidence (KON-fuh-dens)—a feeling or belief that you can do something well

defense (DEE-fens)—the players on a team who try to stop the other team from scoring

interception (in-tur-SEP-shun)—a catch made by a player from the opposing team

offensive (oh-FEN-siv)—relating to the attempt to score in a game

receiving yards (ree-SEE-ving YARDZ)— the distance gained by a player on a passing play

rookie (ROOK-ee)—a first-year player

sack (SAK)—a tackle of the quarterback before he crosses the line of scrimmage

BOOKS

Barrington, Richard. *Tom Brady: Super Bowl Champion.* Living Legends of Sports. New York: Britannica Educational Publishing in association with Rosen Educational Services, 2016.

Cosson, M. J. *Superstars of the Pittsburgh Steelers.* Pro Sports Superstars. Mankato, MN: Amicus, 2014.

Kelley, K. C. *J. J. Watt.* Football Stars Up Close. New York: Bearport Publishing Company, Inc., 2016.

WEBSITES

Football: National Football League
www.ducksters.com/sports/national_football_league.php

NFL Rush
www.nflrush.com

NFL Zone
www.sikids.com/nfl-zone

31

INDEX